BOOB Action

Charles Chiyangwa

ISBN-10: 0984883304
EAN-13: 9780984883301

"Special thanks to the Titty Committee for their endorsement of this book."

TABLE OF CONTENTS

CHAPTER ONE

The foremothers banned thongs!

On a hot summer day, I get up from my usual sitting place to stroll down the Hollywood walk of fame. I have just spent two hours of my life imagining a stand-up comedy performance that will never happen. It makes me feel better though. The only thing that scares me is sometimes it feels like it is really happening. In certain circumstances that whole world becomes me. I speak like someone else. I just say whatever comes to my mind. It gets me in trouble all the time. I cannot help myself.

For now I am going to walk on Hollywood boulevard heading east away from Las Palmas Ave. It is summer time and all the freaks are out. I am now able to take some time off from work because I have ten thousand dollars in my savings account. It has been a long road to get to this point. Precisely ten years since I arrived in Hollywood. Most of my money is earned working as a cashier for a big grocery store located on the corner Melrose Avenue and Vine Street. I have worked there fulltime for a while now. I also have done a variety of small jobs on the side. I used to take old ladies for a walk in the Hollywood hills and get paid for it.

One day I get to a new job and the old lady gets naked. I had to say no I am not here for that. "You are Ryan Steel right?" she said in a sexy voice. "No I am Charles Chiyangwa I am here to take you for a walk down the block" I told her. "Oh Ryan is coming after you then" she said sounding confused. "You might want to consider Ryan's job he gets paid way more than you" she told me while getting dressed. I had no answer to that one. I also moonlighted as a part-time mover. The moving business involves driving big trucks. You are responsible for loading and unloading furniture for rich people who have bought new homes. Taking a refrigerator up some stairs is hard labor. I had to do it in order to survive in this city. It had to be done to keep the dream alive. I work hard at my passions more than other people can endure. Many times I considered taking Ryan's job but never had the courage to do it. Walking down the block with old ladies talking about old Hollywood was good enough for me. It is at the grocery store that I have spent most of my time. Sometimes I am out in the parking lot collecting carts. It is a cat and mouse game with homeless people that somehow want to take the carts off the parking lot. The carts are fitted with a locking system that prevents unauthorized removal from the premises. That does not stop homeless people from trying their luck. Other times I am at the checkout counter bagging groceries. When you do that for eight hours there is no need for a gym. That is a complete workout in itself. The financial rewards have been significant. My life has changed a bit. Just being able to eat out anywhere I want is pretty cool. As a responsible adult I have saved most of my money for a rainy day. I have seen rainy days before and they are not pretty. Sometimes it is pouring rain that gets your underwear wet.

On this beautiful summer day, I am walking down the Boulevard minding my own business. In a dreamlike sequence a drop dead gorgeous African American girl comes out of the store in front of me. She has all the curves of her body in the right places. My first impression is wow that cleavage is something else. She sees the look on my face and plays it up. She surely knows how to tease. I walk a little faster to catch up. She is completely out of my league. That does not matter to me. I thrive on challenges. I present my case to rolling laughter from this girl. She thinks I am the funniest guy she ever met. To be called funny is cool sometimes but not when you are trying to get laid. I ask her why she is alone on a busy summer afternoon. During the summer it is expected that a hot girl like her would be lounging at some pool party somewhere in Hollywood. She tells me she is with her gang. I laugh because I think that is funny. There are no gangsters on Hollywood boulevard. As the conversation goes on I realize I am not getting anywhere with this girl. I just ask for a hug so I could leave her alone. She obliged so she can get rid of me I guess. I put my arms around her. She reacts warmly with a smile. Sometimes I hold too tight. Well I do not have the best of reflexes especially when I get excited. These are things I know I have to work on as my life progresses. One time I held a girl tight and she told me she could hear my heart beating fast. It was not a lie. My heart was beating too fast for real. I almost fainted in her arms. All these thoughts are going through my head and this girl is still in my arms. She gives me a warning that this sought of thing can get me in serious trouble. "Too late now", she raises her angelic voice pushing me away. I look back where she is looking and I cannot believe what I see. Standing there are four fat white guys dressed like gangsters wearing white sneakers blue jeans and oversized white t-shirts. They are accompanied by two thin guys dressed the same. They look very unhappy with me. She walks towards the guys and they move towards me. Two of them are breathing heavy with anger. "Calm down guys I didn't do anything" I am walking backwards looking around. They keep coming and it is clear they are not negotiating anything. "That's my girl you were talking to" one of them said. "Oh no you are too fat for that girl! You need to be working on reducing your doughnut count! You cannot even see your belt! What can you do with that girl? Leave the girl to me. I am a true gangster you are the fat gang" I yell at him. In my head I am like oh my God I cannot believe I said that. The gang starts chasing me on Hollywood boulevard. The only way I am going to live another day is to let my legs carry me as far away from these guys as possible.

I immediately instruct my legs to start the process of saving my life. My legs start running through the crowd looking for an escape route. When your legs are the only thing between you and death strange things happen. I start cheering my own legs. Let's go guys! Lift up guys otherwise this is not going end well! It seems to work in the beginning. Then the two thin guys take over the chase. They are running faster than Kenyans in a marathon. These guys should compete in marathons around the world and give the dominant Kenyans some competition. I am African myself with running in my genes. The thin white guys have the technic of running on a street full of people. They help each other out by letting one of them clear the street. People really start giving them the right of way when they start shouting that I stole their grandmother's purse. It is painful to hear because I am no thief. I cannot stop to defend myself. I manage to stop and shout back. "You stole my doughnuts!" It is becoming increasingly clear that I am going to have some missing teeth at the end of all this. I imagine a few scars to go with it. Chicks are hard to get with missing teeth. I begin to imagine what that would be like. The thin guys got closer to me and one of them grabs my shirt. I immediately stop and push him to the ground. That hard push sent both guys tumbling to the ground. I hear them cry out. They get up fast and are behind me again. My legs start giving me warnings that things are not looking good for me. It feels like a check engine sign flashing. That realization automatically got me in panic mode. I have to think of something before it is too late. How quickly can I think when I am running this fast? A new plan is needed or a disaster of unimaginable proportion is about to unravel. At least that is the way I am looking at it. I am fleeing people that want to break me up into pieces. My legs start to feel very weak. That increases the desire to run faster weird right?

I can feel the wind on my face. Suddenly I stretch my arms out and begin to feel the weightlessness. That is a cool feeling. As I pick up speed my legs start lifting off the ground. God damn I am flying with a broad smile on my face. As I look down at my enemies I can see they are pissed off. They are fuming as they look at me up in the air. "Skeleton man your arms will fall off if you keep running like that" I taunt the two skinny guys. I laugh hard and give them the finger with a smile. That is a big mistake on my part. Never give a finger to someone chasing you. They are not going to say oh he gave us the finger let's go home. They started running like they are in professional competition. I mean the two skinny ones. I can say whatever I want to the fat boys. They can never catch me even after I have run a marathon and had surgery the same day. I am still in flight mode getting worried about how close they are getting to me. I feel my shirt being pulled from behind. That is when I realize I am still on the ground. I am still running if you call it that. I have to let go of a piece of my shirt to break away. I wish I am a bird right now. I can just fly away with no care in the world. Just look for an empty nest and get laid. Yeah birds get laid all the time it is easy for them. Their chicks just fly in and out of the nest and they don't have to do nothing. They do not have to know her name, buy dinner or any of that shit. I realize quickly that I am not a bird but just somebody in real big trouble. Then the thought of God comes to mind. If I see him I think it is the appropriate time to shout, "God damn get me out of here can't you see I am in big trouble?" Then I start thinking about being rescued by firefighters in Los Angeles. If they can rescue a dog in the Los Angeles River they can rescue me. I think maybe I should just call 911. If they ask for my location I can just say I am running on Hollywood Boulevard. Then start running in circles until they arrive. One problem is that they usually come with the police. At this point I can handle talking to the police than being squashed by the three hundred pound guys back there. I am looking to anyone for help. Up ahead I see a strong young woman with muscular arms wearing a sleeveless shirt. I signal for help and she shakes her head with confidence giving me a cold stare. "You are on your own pal", she lets me know moving to the side while passing me. I look back and I see an unbelievable sight. One of the fat guys is running like a football player on his way to scoring a touchdown. He overtakes the two skinny guys like they are walking. This is a surprise because I did not know fat people can run like that.

Finally I remembered that I always carry a dart case given to me by my elders when I left Africa. The elders included my dad and they were concerned about violence in America. They prepared poisonous darts for me to defend myself if ever my life is in danger. It is a bag full of black magic weapons including bows and arrows. I carried all of that on the plane. It was before 911 happened. I really never intended to use them. My idea was to one day go to the sea and dump them out there. The silver case decorated with embroidery black and white beads carries the poisonous darts. Included with the darts is a disguise cigar type device to blow them at unsuspecting enemies. I always carry that small dart case with me everywhere I go. The elders spent a good deal of time explaining to me what the darts are meant to do. Out of all those explanations all I remember is that the effects are temporary. They end when the person is no longer a threat to me. The other thing I remember is that the poison makes people do different things. They gave me the list. I did not take them seriously so I threw the list away.

I am too tired to keep running, so I am going to take care of this problem once and for all. I get to Hollywood and Vine and made a left to avoid crowds at the train station. I patiently wait in the alley, and as the fat guy runs past me I blow one on him. I immediately come out to the street and openly challenge him to a fight. The whole gang look relieved because finally one of their own is now going to get a chance to crush me for my alleged crime. I have everybody on one side so that I do not get surrounded. The African American girl arrives and joins her gang. They are all cheering for the fat gangster. I dance around to waste time so the poison can take effect. At one point I do the Bruce Lee walk, the occasional nose swipe and a karate pose. He slightly shakes his head and makes a howling sound. It goes from howling to fight me to weird head movements. The tactic is a big surprise for the gang. They all look at each other shaking their heads feeling really sorry for me. Then he goes to straight up howling and barking like a dog. Things take a dramatic turn when he goes down on his knees, trying to bite me like a dog. The gang is puzzled by this development. I sucker punch him and he goes down. He rolls over like a dog and back on his fours barking like a fighting dog. At this point I feel it is safe to slowly walk away. When the thin guys try to follow me, I point to their barking friend. They all retreat to help their colleague. I can see them trying to stand him up. He walks a few steps and barks like a dog again. I know I got him. The good thing is that he is going to be okay. This on condition he is no longer a danger to me.

I walk away from the scene towards Sunset Boulevard. Miss beautiful calls me back. As soon as I hear her angelic voice I stop to think of my next move. My mind flashes a million times trying to come up with ideas to turn this situation around. I do not turn back right away. Her angelic voice grows angry and angrier as she gets closer to me. Even to a person like me who has been called names before, this is over the line. I turn back with a smile to try and calm the situation down. She is so angry she slaps me very hard and I fall to the ground. While on the ground and in pain I have to figure out an appropriate response. I get up pretending nothing has happened to me and everything is okay. With a smile on my face I start talking to her. Before I can finish the first word she spits right into my eyes. What do you do when you have been spit on by the most beautiful girl in the world? If you are me you put your tongue out and lick your lips. That is a nice move with the right timing. Just as I am licking my lips the gang is standing behind her. They are witnesses to the spectacle. To my surprise they seem to think the whole thing is amusing. The angry gang is laughing. It looks like I am out of trouble and it is time to leave this scene. Amidst the laughing I try to slip away. I do not get far they quickly capture me. They drag me back into the alley and a small crowd of on-lookers gather around the entrance to the al-ley. They immediately push me to the ground. The gang holds me face down while talking to Miss beautiful. They ask her whether she wants to do it or not. She lets them know she is ready. Now I am thinking she is going to shoot me dead. I hear the click sound of a revolver and I start to prey. They turn me over so I can see her shoot me. A clear plastic bag covers two members of the gang holding me down to avoid blood on them.

The gang secures me facing up and one guy's hand is firmly on my privates. He squeezes them hard making me cry out opening my mouth wide. A surreal scene begins to unfold as I scream in pain. The girl with the voice of an angel walks over me and urinates into my mouth. Closing my mouth is not going to help me. I have never tasted girl urine before. Well small traces of it maybe. This is a large amount. I did not know girls can carry that much urine in them. She looks into my eyes with a sense of accomplishment and walks away. There is a burning sensation in my eyes causing cloudy vision. A good size crowd gathers and it clearly becomes a laughing my ass off afternoon for them. At least I cannot clearly see the faces of the people laughing. A couple of guys unzip their pants so they can urinate on me as well. I get up and disappear around the corner. She caught me by surprise. Honestly my skin cannot take any more urine period. The only light side of this ordeal is that I got to see her vagina. It was clear she had not shaved in a while. All I could see was hair. This time the face did not match the carpet. This carpet is long. It serves the purpose of a sprinkler I guess. What the hell was that? Is she just lazy? One of my ex- girlfriends once told me that it is time consuming to shave.

At the end of the day a girl has urinated on me. That is the only thing that matters. I wonder what the forefathers could have done about this sought of behavior. I guess they did not care about such things. They probably could have laughed about it over a beer or something. The foremothers could have taken strong action against this girl. While the forefathers were busy writing the constitution and other popular stuff, the foremothers did the dirty jobs for them. The foremothers did not want their daughters wearing thongs. They passed legislation banning the thong. Girls who had their tongues pierced and had tattoos were sent to prison back then. The foremothers did good stuff as well they banned prostitution, and ushered in the one man one woman rule. History never gives them credit because of the other controversial stuff they did. Yeah right!

How am I going to explain this whole thing to my children or grandchildren? Grandpa will try to explain but I will not tell the whole story. I will leave out the part where my stomach was hit, and I swallowed a good chunk of the girl's urine. All the other things that this girl did to me shall remain untold. Everybody has untold stories or untold parts of stories. There are parts of this story that will remain untold. Maybe that is why I am obsessed with cologne. I always wear the coolest and most expensive cologne. When I put my game on the first complement I get is you smell nice.

Okay here is the version of events my kids will get to hear. When I was young before I met your mom, I used to be a player. I parked my Lamborghini on Hollywood boulevard, and met this young and beautiful African American girl. She liked playing around so she started chasing me and her cousins followed. They chased me laughing and playing on Hollywood boulevard. I pushed one of her cousins down and she continued chasing me off the boulevard. In the end she got a water gun and sprayed me with water. I was glad because it was a hot summer day. Moral of the story is I was a player. Your mom was really lucky she was able to tie me down.

CHAPTER TWO

There is a stripper pole on the subway train.

The next day I decide to go downtown Los Angeles for a change of environment. I have not been to downtown Los Angeles since the L.A Live Entertainment complex was opened. I am sure now is a good time to check it out. I make my way to the Hollywood and Highland complex to board the redline subway train towards downtown. The entrance to the trains is on Hollywood boulevard which is a hive of activity most of the day. At this point in the afternoon all the characters that parade Hollywood boulevard are out to play. From Superman, Sponge Bob, Wonder Woman and Shrek can all be seen taking pictures with tourists. I love this area of Hollywood. My frequent visits here led to the best of random times. That is how I got to meet Wonder Woman. After a lot of futile attempts to get laid by a celebrity I started looking for alternatives. Apparently celebrities want to have sex with other famous people. That is lame to me. What fun is there in doing that? Sleep with an ordinary person. Make a difference in somebody's life.

I finally settled on celebrity lookalikes. They have an open door policy or should I say open leg policy. The male celebrity lookalikes just take any sexual favors offered to them by desperate women. Believe me they do get some offers. No disrespect to the legends of Hollywood, but they got some serious competition from some of these characters. The Wonder Woman on Hollywood boulevard now is better than the original. That is not a fair comparison because I was not around when the original Wonder Woman was doing her thing. If a girl walks into my bedroom wearing that costume she is Wonder Woman. I will give her all the time she needs to perform her wonders. At this point I start to imagine her doing all the poses. I just relax on the bed then shout softly to be saved. After I had a piece of Wonder Woman ass I was left wondering. What else is out there? Some of these celebrity lookalikes taste just as good as the real thing. After Wonder Woman I went after Super Girl and taped her ass too. I just said to myself I love this town!

Oh! I almost forgot I have somewhere to go. I go down the escalators a few times before getting to the boarding zone. As I go down the escalators a cold breeze hits me. I think it is part of the cooling system for the metro station. They did a good job. The electronic monitor says the train is arriving in five minutes. As I wait around for the train to arrive a woman about 30 years old caught my eye. She is conservatively dressed in a dark blue skirt suit with nice shoes, and a light blue church type hat. She has the single mother look or married at least. She appears to be wondering around looking for something on the ground. She approaches a couple of people and appears to be explaining something to them. They have some type of conversation before she goes on with her business. She comes towards me and asks for a dollar. I politely tell her I do not have any money. She becomes angry and furious. I do not understand why someone I do not know is mad at me for not giving her a dollar. It is not like everyone is giving her some money.

She starts accusing me of fathering her kids. According to her we have three kids together and I am not taking care of them. I have never met this woman in my life. It creates an amusing situation for other passengers waiting for the train. Here I am denying allegations of fathering three kids by a woman I have never met before. Two very muscular men in track suit bottoms and tank tops get off of the elevator. They walk towards the edge of the platform close to where I am standing. They stand next to us waiting for the train. One of the muscular guys is more feminine in his mannerisms and the way he talks. He takes an interest in what the crazy woman is saying to me. He makes very animated reactions to her allegations. At some point I stop replying the crazy woman just praying for the train to arrive. The train arrives and I immediately jump on board. She does not get on the train which is a big sigh of relief for me.

For the next thirty seconds or so while the train doors are still open, she just shouts at me. "Take care of your kids! Three kids, what am I supposed to do while you are gone? Jason seven years old needs you!" She shouts a lot of things and the passengers' attention shift towards me. She becomes more hyper and starts humping. "This is all you like" she yells pointing at me. "You want every woman! If you are a woman on this train beware of this cock-roach! He will get on you! He used me and he will use you too!" The doors finally close and I am glad the nightmare is finally over. The train takes off and there is some awkward silence on the train. I look around and realize every-body is looking at me. I honestly do not know what it all means. One of the muscular guys confronts me on why I am not taking care of my kids. I told him and everyone on the train that I have no wife and no kids. The muscular guys get very angry with me. They think I am making fun of them in front of the crowd. They immediately hold me one on each arm. There is no way I can break free. They invite any passenger to come out and punch me for not taking care of my kids.

A seventy five year old Hispanic lady gets up and addresses everyone. She tells a poignant story of how she was left by her husband to fend for herself and her son. She looks at me with evil eyes while she talks. She explains how her son now fifty years old was shot because of an absent father. Her son suffered some brain damage and is sitting next to her. She announces that she wants to be the first to hit me to everyone's applause. That put a smile on my face because I have nothing to worry about. I am actually worried she is going to hurt herself trying to hit me. She walks slowly from her sit doing some cool karate moves. She strikes me in the stomach, while making the same exact moves Jackie Chan did in the classic movie Drunken Master. The crowd cheers for her to do more and she delivers with a blow to my face. The old lady's blow shakes my brains loose. I begin to see things in slow motion. It takes about a minute for the world to move at regular speed. The hard punch in my stomach feels like I have been hit by an iron bar. I do not make a sound pretending it does not hurt at all. After a few good punches the sound of someone hurting naturally comes out to everyone's applause. She comes close to my face and asks if I am now going to take care of my kids. I just nod my head in agreement. I cannot talk. Her strong punches make me think maybe this old lady used to be a marine or some type of soldier. A line just keeps coming to my head. Do not mess with grandma! The old lady starts doing her Drunken Master moves again. I close my eyes and scream to scare her. It turns out she is just making a bow marking the end of her routine. Her disabled son indicates he wants to be part of the fun. She tells everyone he is a big fan of wrestling, and wants to sit on me or give me a close line. The muscular guys secure me on the floor of the train and her son sits on my head giggling.

I cannot figure out what is worse his ass on my head or the smell. He is just basically dropping his body weight on me pulling my leg up. They pull me up to answer some more questions. The old lady returns and demands an apology from me for not taking care of my kids. At this point I can no longer deny it. I do exactly what every reasonable guy would do. I apologize for not taking care of kids I do not have. I take advantage of my acting skills and become emotional in my apology. I appeal to my son Jason to forgive me.

After my apology I notice two police deputies in the next trailer. I rush to them for help. They immediately accompany me back and I explain to them what happened to me. I point directly at the old lady as the attacker. I tell the police the muscular guys held me down while she beat me up. They all deny it. I point out the son for sitting on me. He just pulls a bunch of medical records out. The police deputies just shake their heads. When I first pointed at the old lady as the attacker one of the officers actually laughed. Then a wise ass stands up and tells the deputies that nothing happened to me. He tells the deputies that I stood up and apologized for things I did wrong in life. He then pulls video from his iPhone. The video shows me apologizing and no one is holding me. Yes no one is holding me. They let go of me once I started apologizing. That is too much for the police to take. At the next stop they order me out of the train back to my kids, or get arrested for making false statements to the police. I make the choice to go and attend to my kids.

I get off the train at the Wilshire and Vermont Avenue station. I get out of the subway station to get some air while walking around the corner of Wilshire Boulevard and Vermont Avenue. There are some shops and apartments above the subway station. It is a high foot traffic area. There is a Shell gas station across the street from the train station. I have to wait for another train to complete my trip. Wondering aimlessly around the intersection does not help the way I feel right now. All bets are off with old ladies. If one of them thinks they can fight me I am ready to bring them down. They lose their old lady status if they punch like a teenage black belt.

I ride the escalators back down to the boarding zone to complete my trip. In two minutes the train arrives and I hop on. I immediately realize they have a stripper pole on the train. How did I miss this? It is right there in the center for all to see and use. That gets me thinking the trains are not in operation from like midnight to five in the morning. If they park these trains in a tunnel going through the middle of a mountain somewhere, there may be parties going on during the night. Parties I do not know about. The whole thing unfolds in my head. A whole train full of strippers and music as loud as can be. If the train parks in the middle of the mountain no sound goes out to the public. Yes I can see it, free flowing liquor, naked girls, dirty dancing and lap dances. Wow! what a world that could be. I want to be part of it! I start hearing that strip club voice speaking. "Ladies and gentleman please welcome the subway girls! Please welcome to the stage Kandy! I am thinking this is the people's train they cannot be doing this kind of thing at night. I am holding on to the pole with this wide grin on my face, like a teenager that has been kissed by a girl for the first time. I quickly take my hand off the pole because of the unsanitary nature of stripper poles. Well it depends on who is stripping. When some girls strip I am licking that pole.

As I slowly come back to reality I open my eyes. I see a young man in the front extending his hand offering me a seat. It is the vertical single sit reserved for the disabled or the elderly. The sit happens to be empty. I slowly sit down fidgeting trying to get my headphones out so I can listen to music and avoid conversation. Then the kind young man begins to speak to me. I quickly realize that the young man is a military veteran. He tells me his name is Chad Robertson. Chad is a fit Caucasian male about twenty years old. The thing about people that have served in the military is that they always tell you upfront how many years they served, where they were stationed, and whether or not they were deployed in a war situation. One other thing that is always present about the veterans is the pride they all have for saving their country. In Chad's case he tells me he was trained at Camp Pendleton California and was deployed in Afghanistan. Chad did one tour of duty that went horribly wrong and left him at war with himself. I quickly realize that Chad is one of those vets coming from Afghanistan with some type of ailment. I have not met a vet with any condition before so I do not know what it looks like. He begins to speak with me and tells me that the war is still going on which is true. He then goes on to tell me that we are not safe on the train. The Taliban can come and get us. He makes me listen to the sound of gunfire he is hearing. I am only hearing the sound of a moving train. He becomes animated responding to the sounds he is hearing. Chad makes it clear that whatever happens he will protect me. For me to continue having a civil conversation with him, I have to agree that the war is still going on, and that we are in immediate danger on the train. As I look into his eyes I begin to feel his pain. When he is mellow his charismatic personality comes back to charm everyone around him. The polite young man that offered me a seat is the real Chad. I see the struggles of a young man who wants to be normal just like me. I cannot help but think this is the new war. This is what happens when a country spends a decade fighting two wars on foreign lands. The war comes home and ordinary people like me are left with the duty of living with the consequences of the wars. That includes taking care of the wounded warriors as they adjust to a new normal. The war for ordinary people living in America is just beginning, as the troops begin to come home. Chad goes on high alert looking around like he is hearing something. He tells me that he is ready to fight the Taliban wherever they are. Chad is ready to protect me and others in this ongoing war. He reminds me that people do not understand what kind of danger they are in. It is clear that Chad still wants to serve his country. He still wants to help others. He feels he is still on duty. I know at this point it is Chad who needs my help. I have no idea how to help him. The intercom announces my stop and I start getting ready to leave. I stand up feeling my body shiver with emotion and my eyes filling with tears. I thank Chad for protecting me and for being a good guy. The train stops and the doors open. I walk out of the train with a heavy heart. I turn back to have a last look at Chad as I feel a warm tear run down my right cheek. The train leaves the 7th and Metro station as I make my way to the escalator.

CHAPTER THREE

Miss Liquor and Mr. Beer hook up.

I get upstairs at the 7th and Metro station and catch the blue line train to long beach. The blue line is the one that stops at the Staples Centre. As I am walking to L.A Live I notice there are some recently built apartments scattered around the area. It is quite remarkable what has been done to this part of downtown Los Angeles. Suddenly something jumps out of the first floor balcony about 6 to 8 feet up on to the street. It lands right behind me and it scares the shit out of me. This kind of shit makes you pee in your pants. This is downtown Los Angeles and I have no idea how good the place has been changed. They said in the news the revitalization of downtown Los Angeles has been achieved. I have no clue how everything worked out.

To say I am scared would be an understatement. My mind races back and forth with my adrenalin kicking in immediately. The relief is that a seemly hot white girl is behind me. She is laughing at me for being scared. I stop and ask her an honest question. Do you know this is not funny? She looks at me and laughs hysterically. Then she tells me she has been doing it for years and nobody gets scared. The men she surprises are busy looking at her ass. I have to let her know right away that I am African. We surprise the animals and the animals do not surprise us. When we get surprised that is a whole new ball game. My reflexes are dangerous and deadly to other human beings. I can run so fast in these types of situations I can disappear in thin air. If anyone gets in my way I knock them down and it feels like they have been hit by a car.

I stop walking to tell her women have fucked up my life. I do not want to have anything to do with beautiful women at least for now. Hot booty shaking women have contributed to all my problems. Jumping out of balconies is frowned upon in my world. She looks at me and tells me she is not going to get me in trouble. "I am going to blow your mind babe get ready" she declares in her soft sexy voice. That makes me think. Wait a minute, there is nothing wrong with a beautiful girl blowing my mind. I scan her from head to toe and it is safe to say by my standards she is a bombshell. My standards are pretty low most girls qualify. She is wearing tight fitting dark pink trainers accentuating her ass, light pink tank top and white sneakers. She has a nice God given ass. I mean every man's dream ass. I cannot help but notice her flat chest. The thing is I have a lot to work with on this girl. A somewhat flat chest does not matter. To be fair when I checked out her much talked about ass. I made the w-o-h-o-o-o African appreciation of ass chant. Yes when I see nice booty I chant. When I see boobs a lot of stories have been told about that. Her booty is now my business. I quickly find out her name is Taylor Green. Together we walk towards the L.A Live Entertainment complex. Taylor is 5'7 tall hard body type chick with blonde hair and brown eyes. She is a fine ass white girl to me. As an African I am used to getting fat white chicks. That is my birth right. Somehow she gets all interested in my African stories about lions and hyenas. I have to make up some of the stories after I run out of the good ones.

We end up at the ESPN sports zone bar and restaurant at LA Live. I get some drinks and a bite to eat for both of us. While waiting for the food and drinks, Taylor shows me pictures of her sister Lauren on her iPhone. She looks amazing. Taylor downs a few tequila shots. The liquor starts talking to me. We all know how Miss Liquor is outspoken and blunt. She spills the beans on how Lauren got to look the way she does on the iPhone pictures. She is not ashamed of anything her sister did to earn her boobs. Miss liquor tells me straight up that she is looking for someone to pay for her breast implants. In return she will fall in love with the guy. Miss liquor goes on about how she will treat the person willing to pay for the missing part of her body. I am drinking too and Mr. Beer talks about how much money he has saved up the past ten years. Apparently Mr. Beer is willing to pay for Miss Liquor's cosmetic surgery. Mr. Beer asks for a sample from Miss Liquor. That request sends the new couple meandering arm in arm back to Miss Liquor's apartment. Well after Mr. Beer samples Miss Liquor's asserts, it is the best sample he has ever had. So as the story goes Mr. Beer agrees to pay for Miss Liquor's breast implants with some of the money from his savings. Mr. Beer pays seven thousand out of ten thousand dollars in his savings account. Mr. Beer after sampling Miss Liquor goes on her computer, types and prints out the BOOB ACTION CONTRACT. Miss Liquor signs the contract with no problems. The contract has one hundred enforceable provisions. It includes a clause that she cannot go out with another man for two years. Another clause prohibits any other man from touching the new boobs except a doctor. The most interesting clause gives Mr. Beer the right to touch the boobs on demand. In the event of a breach of contract by Miss Liquor her sister Lauren takes over her responsibilities as enshrined in the contract. The last provision includes the removal of the implants by force or coercion in the event of a serious breach of the contract. Miss Liquor signs the contract after receiving a hundred bucks signing bonus from Mr. Beer. They both sleep at her apartment downtown Los Angeles. The next morning they drink some more and make their way to the plastic surgeon's office. Mr. Beer pays the money and surgery is scheduled for Miss Liquor.

Taylor emerges from surgery with a clean bill of health. We are definitely going to get married and live happily ever after. Apparently many people are thinking about marrying her too. People come out of the woodworks. From homeless guys to celebrity lookalikes all want a piece of the action. She now attracts the attention of old seniors to hot blooded teenagers who just want her clothes off right away. You can call me naive but I think since I am the creator of this fantasy I own it. Taylor is bound to recognize my contributions and abide by the contract. I have listened to the

President of The United States saying this is a country of laws many times. She has to abide by the contract we mutually signed otherwise all contracts signed in this country are invalid. I can accept an out of court settlement, where I take her to a secluded island resort for a week. One week in a hotel room with access to my boob creation settles the whole thing for me. I have made the suggestion and she thinks it is a joke. The expensive cars she now rides in, and the fast life is just too much for her to deal with me. I am in a situation an African guy cannot win. I decided to go back to her apartment and talk to her. The talks did not go well to say the least. She mooned me and told me to kiss her natural ass. In a good relationship I seriously consider such requests. It is the sight of her natural ass and my boobs that gets me. God must have created her ass on a good day and fell asleep while doing her boobs. That is why I had to help out.

It is mid-morning downtown Los Angles, I just walked out of Taylor's apartment making my way back to the train station. As I am walking down the street, I see a group of young hard core Hispanic gangsters' blocking my way. I continue to walk towards them. "Hey that's the dude sleeping with your girl" one of them shouts pointing at me. I look back it looks like I am surrounded. I have no choice but to turn into the alley. I run as fast as I can and hope the police show up. I do not go very far because more gangsters appear in front of me in the alley. This is a coordinated ambush of some sort. They close in on me and I get pushed into the wall. "You are fucking my girl ha! You are fucking my girl ha!" the gang leader says repeatedly. I can feel the gun hitting the back of my head. It smells like it has just been fired too. The other gangsters encourage him to shoot me. "Let me give this to the new guy. You want to be part of us? This will make you part of us" he gives the gun to a younger gangster. He pulls out another revolver from the back of his pants. I start hearing small screams and heavy things falling down. "Who the hell is that?" the leader asks his boys. There is no answer. "The war is still going on and the Taliban will die today" a voice that sounds very familiar screams. I know exactly who that is. Chad beats up most of the gangsters and they flee the scene. "Let him go or you are a dead man", Chad orders the leader holding me. He starts hitting me in the head with the gun again. Chad gets to him and hacks him down. He gets up and runs away with Chad in pursuit. The gang leader turns back and fires two shots into chad's stomach area. Chad tumbles to the ground and I have to take cover behind a huge green trash bin. After the gangsters disappear, I run to Chad laying there motionless near a puddle of water from the gutters. "Chad! Chad! Get up!" I shout turning him over. His eyes are wide open and he begins to speak. "The war is still going on and you need to protect yourself at all times", he says. He pulls both of the bullets from his bulletproof vest and shakes his head. "The war is still going on and you need to understand that", he tells me again. "I understand thank you man", as I help him get up. We start walking to the pavement. He orders me to walk behind him, as we tip toe to the corner as soldiers do in a war situation. We finally get to the end of the alley. He checks both directions and then gives me an all clear to go on the street. Chad has just saved my life in spectacular fashion.

CHAPTER FOUR

When the famous white light comes to take me I will switch it off.

I nearly lost my life because of Taylor. Where do I go from here? I have lost seven thousand dollars and all I have to show for it is a stupid contract. Contracts are enforced by the courts, so I have to see a lawyer and get it all figured out. The lawyers I am going to see are located in a high rise building on Wilshire Boulevard in the miracle mile area. The company's name is The Law Offices of Mitch and Schuster. I meet with Mitch one of the partners. I explain my story the best way I can. First of all he tells me the contract is null and void. This is because of the simple fact the contract was signed while we were all drunk. Mitch advises me that I can sue her for emotional distress, for any future inheritance she might have since she is broke.

I let Mitch know that my interests are not monetary. I want Taylor to comply with the contract. The minute I make my feelings about the money situation known the mood changes in the office. He now wants me out of his office and threatens to charge me if I do not leave. Most of the lawyers I call think it is a joke. It is clear the only option left for me is the removal of the implants by force or coercion. How is that going to happen? Do I even have the balls to pull off something like that on someone I like? I am still in love with this woman. The prospect of using force weighted heavily on me. I try hard to get it out of my mind and move on. People keep asking me what I am going to do with my savings. Every time that happens the anger comes back like it never left. The urge to do something comes back with a vengeance. How could this have happened to me? I am an honest guy trying to make a decent living in the city of Angels. It is really hard to comprehend my situation.

Clearly I am still in love with a woman who has moved on. She has done so with seven thousand dollars of my money and cleavage to die for. I feel like I have been robbed. It is worse when you are robbed with a smile. This girl acts like it is normal to get seven thousand dollars for a boob job and disappear. Just like a bank robber feels it is normal to rob a bank of a million bucks and hope that nobody notices.

In the contract it says if Taylor is in breach, her sister Lauren takes over her duties. Lauren had her boobs done a year ago. They look amazing that is why I put her name in the contract. I had to insure my money in case things went wrong. Now things have gone wrong and according to the contract it is time for her to step in. Taylor is supposed to have told her sister Lauren about the contract. You do not suddenly wake up with new boobs without people asking you how you got them. This is especially true if you are an unemployed crack head with no income.

According to her sister Lauren has a tasty tongue. She works at Hooters in Santa Monica that is her boobs for a buck job. I have been to Hooters the girls are very talkative and expressive. If I am going to approach her I better have my A- game on. My B- game cannot do it. That brings my friend Mike in the mix. Mike is a light skinned African American brother I met when I first moved to Los Angeles years ago. He is a wannabe rapper whose rapping is kind of off. He has zero street credibility. He tells people he has been in prison, but to the best of my knowledge he watches a lot of Lockup Raw on MSNBC. He watches prison stories on television. He can go toe to toe with a guy coming out of prison, and can make people believe he did some time. Mike smokes a lot of weed and when he talks his sentences end like a rap song. His upper body is all covered in tattoos. He has a medium body not very muscular. His game with the ladies is pretty good. I have seen him get laid many times with girls out of his league. I do not know any girl who can say no when Mike tells them he just signed a record deal. He gets laid and disappears in thin air. According to him when you fuck a girl it is for life. She cannot rub it off. He got mad at me when I told him that when a girl has had you it is for life too. She can walk away just like we can. I know that from experience.

I call Mike for some help. Together we have to go to Hooters in Santa Monica and talk to Lauren. I write down everything for Mike and we rehearse it. I drive him to Santa Monica. We get there and go inside Hooters. With my blessing Mike has the power to finish the negotiations and set up a meeting at a later date. At that meeting I can be given access to the girls for the first time. Mike starts the monologue on point. I remain close so I can hear him talking. He speaks to Lauren right away. ''The reason I am here is because my boy over there is your sister's boyfriend. He got your sister those boobs you know what I am saying. They signed a contract that gave him ownership of the boobs. Your sister is now with some rich white guy. In the contract you know what I am saying. You are listed as the person to take over the contract when your sister is in breach. Your sister is in breach of the contract. According to the contract my boy is supposed to start feeling these you know what I'm saying. He wants to know when you are off work, so you two can get together you know what I'm saying. He is a good guy''. I am thinking this is pretty good more than I expected from Mike. "Are you kidding me?" Lauren asks trying to understand Mike. She asks Mike how much her sister was paid. He tells her seven thousand bucks. Lauren asks how much she is getting from the deal. Mike explains to her that her sister has to cut her some money from what she got. That is the last thing I heard from the conversation. The staff asks me to move because the table I am at has customers coming to it. A few minutes later Mike comes back to me and we step outside Hooters. Mike tells me that Lauren wants her own contract for six thousand dollars before any meeting.

"Hey man I want to tell you something. Give me a chance let me tell you the truth man"

Mike appears fed up. He starts to speak and I listen. "You know man I want to be honest with you man. You are not going to have Lauren. That contract is a piece of shit. You know what I am saying. You got robbed by Taylor and you have to learn to live with it man. Lauren did not even know about the contract. She does not even know you. She only heard her sister mention your name once. Taylor described you as some fool she met last night. It is over man you know what I am saying. This is Los Angeles man. Find yourself another girl and forget about these bitches. Let's roll some weed man and forget about this whole thing" Mike walks away. After Mike said that everything became very clear to me. If there is a path to get that money Mike could have been on it like that. He smells money better than prostitutes. At this point I am convinced that I have lost my money. All I can do is try to manage my disaster.

These overwhelming feelings are getting me to dark places. It takes me back to how I felt when I got hit by a truck back in Zimbabwe. I am probably one of a few people in the world to be hit by a truck and live to tell about it. That experience changed my perceptions about life and about my family. I had a chance to see my own funeral, or at least a glimpse of what it would look like if the lord had taken me that night. When people leave this earth they have no idea how people react to their passing on. They have no idea how much people really cared for them. At least I know my family cried like little babies. I had a chance to see their reactions to what was thought to be my last moments or hours on earth. I had about seven minor accidents with some bike riders in my childhood. Those always ended at the local clinic. When you get hit by a truck, it usually ends with you at the morgue with a tag on one of your feet. That tag will have your name on it. I can just visualize myself complain about the cold in the morgue. It is cold get me out of here! Put me in the ground or wherever burn me! It is too cold in this motherfucker! I do not understand this, people spend their whole lives damaging the environment making the weather hot, and the last place they put people when they die is in a freezer.

Instead of the mortuary I found myself strapped to a gurney and saw my family cry for me. That experience was too traumatic for me. I had been to many funerals for my family members who wasted away from disease. My mind keeps going back to a few seconds after I was hit by the truck. The truck driver did not even stop. It is not clear if the driver knew he had hit someone or not. At the end of the fucking day all I know is he did not stop. I lay on the side of the road. I could see my two brothers crying looking at me as I lay on the ground. I could not hear a sound and my eyes were fixed at the night sky. Then I started to hear a soothing catholic symphony playing in the background. It was peaceful. I remember trying to find a way to breathe. My body was in some kind of paralysis. I knew what I wanted to do. I wanted to breathe but nothing was happening. I kept thinking this is not the end of me. I want to go to Hollywood someday. I have to breathe and breathe now. Those few moments that I could not breathe were the most terrifying moments in my life. I could feel the paralysis wave moving through my body as if certain organs were beginning to shut down. I had to somehow get out of it. I started to see two beams of light. It sounded like a car stopping to see what had happened but I was not sure. This could be the famous white light coming to get me. Terrifying does not describe how I felt at that moment. I have always told friends that if ever the white light comes to get me I would switch it off. I never imagined it would feel like the way it did. At that point I think I fought the biggest fight of my life. I gagged and got my breath back. Those few first gasps of air I took were like heaven. It was hard breathing but it was breathing. I was alive. A passerby that stopped drove me to my house less than a mile away. Why did they take me to the house not the emergency room? I do not understand that logic up to this day. I was in Zimbabwe and I survived the ordeal.

I feel like a superhero though I have no powers. Well if I have powers I can just use them to get laid anyway. Having the power to go to the mall and point at a girl you lets go. I can just imagine how much trouble that can cause in my life. I am cool with no powers.

We got to my house and I was still in a trance state. I could see a parade of my loved ones crying as they looked at me. I could not help but ask questions in my mind. Why do people cry so loud? You are going to lose your voice. I saw my mom bang her head on the wall. I wanted to say mom stop that. You do not have health insurance. That shit is going to hurt later. Here is the thing, when you get hit by a truck you do not expect to survive. People do not expect you to survive. I looked okay. People were told I had been hit by a truck. What that meant to them was that at some point I was going to die. My high school ex-girlfriend came over and told me I gave her the best sex ever. Who knew? That is my first vote for the sexiest man alive contest.

An ambulance was called and I was strapped to a gurney and taken to the hospital. We got to the hospital and the nurse had big boobs. I immediately got an erection and at that point I knew I was going to make it. I had a reason to live and nobody was going to stop me. The doctor finally came to see me after waiting for more than an hour. He was concerned that I might have internal bleeding. I was afraid of being cut up. I looked the doctor in the eye, and told him all my blood was flowing in its correct veins. I could feel it. I had no internal bleeding at all. He looked at me and smiled. He started counting my ribs back and forth. He then placed his finger between one of them. The doctor held out his hand, and called for the nurse who immediately brought him an empty syringe. He took the syringe and put it where his finger was. Before I could ask what was going on he pushed the needle right through my ribs. He pulled part of the syringe out like sucking out something in me. He immediately pulled the needle out, and informed me there was no internal bleeding. I looked at him like I just told you that. Sometimes doctors need to listen to their patients. My blood has been running through my body for decades now. I can tell when it is off course. His answer was that I was in shock. I was in shock that he put a needle into my chest. I had told him point blank that I had no internal bleeding. He came back an hour later with a paper for me to sign. This was just in case they had to do surgery on my shoulder. He was talking about the shoulder that got hit by the truck. I refused to sign. He told me I could die then I signed.

When I was being moved around in a wheelchair I discovered a problem a few people talk about. I discovered that my face is at the same level with people's butts. When they pass gas I was in the line of fire. I was able to tell what people had eaten from their gas. I encountered one of the most horrific smells in my life from a man wearing a suit in front of me. I think he had eaten a rotten dead cat or some rotten dead wild animal or something. I remember getting very animated gasping for fresh air. He made me very angry. I peddled the wheelchair fast with one hand and rear ended him. He turned back and tried to talk to me. I could not open my mouth to such a smell. I just kept pointing at him. I requested a surgical musk to protect me from gas. Next time you pass gas in a public area look around; if there is a wheelchair nearby please hold your fire until they pass.

The next morning the most unbelievable scene unfolded. The doctors did what seemed like hundreds of tests. It was determined that I was in deed one of the luckiest people in the world. The only thing that was wrong with me was my dislocated shoulder which they had already popped back in. With only a sling on my right arm and some bruises I was discharged the next day. My journey from the hospital back to the house become one of the most emotional moments of my life. I came out of that experience knowing that my family loves me. Their love is unconditional love. To think my life could have ended like that scares me. All the dreams flashed out. I am glad my life did not end that way. I was given a second chance. At the back of my mind I know I am a man on a mission. I just do not know what the mission is. Maybe the mission is to entertain people around the world. I am just going to keep doing things that excite me and see what happens.

Boobs excite me and that is a good thing. For a while every time I met people driving any type of truck I clinched my fists ready to fight them. I just wanted them to say something and just go off on them. I had to learn to calm myself down. I discovered that whenever I laid my eyes on a pair of boobs it calmed me down. Just like weed I mellow and calm down. This was years ago before the boob incident on Hollywood boulevard happened. I have a history with boobs. They bring pleasure and pain. I am happy to take both.

At the moment I am receiving the pain part of the deal. I paid for them but I cannot have them. Another sad part of my story is that I did not willingly drop the comedy microphone. If it was up to me I would be on a stage near your town today doing stand-up comedy. That was not to be due to a series of events beyond my control. Honestly I think my ouster from the stage was like someone coming to you in the middle of a stand-up performance, and pointing a gun to your head. Then giving you a choice to stand down or have your brains blown off in front of the audience. I chose to live that is why I am able to tell my story today. It is one thing to have a gun to your head and the choice is be funny or die. I could have lived with that because I can be funny. Get the hell out of here or die is what I still struggle with today. That is how it felt like then and that is how it feels like now. I try to live just like everybody else. The nature of my being takes over and I cannot control what happens. In between the action is the grits of a tormented comedic soul. A life that could have been. A life like no other. This is a life that could have been taken away, and have always been spared by God. I never ask why because I am still standing. Here I stand to pee on all the haters.

After the Taylor episode in my life I decided to seek professional help. This is because the alto ego I created to fantasize about my failed stand-up comedy career is taking over my life. It is beginning to make important decisions for me. I want that to end. I want to be me again. I want to solve problems on my own.

I have decided to see a shrink to take care of my problems. The one I am going to see is a young lady who just graduated from Harvard University. She has been in business for about a year. Outside her office is where I am. I am looking at the marquee with her name Shaunda Williams on it. Suddenly I begin to feel light headed. I sit down on a bus stop bench in front of her office. A conversation starts between me and a voice in my head. The voice of the alto ego I created. The alto ego is beginning to take over my life. The fucker has been making important decisions with real consequences. That is why I am at the shrink's office to get help. **You want to get rid of me. That's why you are here**. No I am here to get my priorities right. **Don't be smart with me. I know you are here to get rid of me. This is so you can think on your own. You have**

not been doing a good job. Look I want to be able to think straight. **I have been doing that for you. I have helped you all this time now you want to get rid of me. Look I am Charles Chiyangwa bitch. I am the real thing deal with it. You are weak and you don't know what you are doing**. No I am Charles Chiyangwa and I know what I am doing. **You had never been with a Miss World type chick before. I gave you a fine chick and you never even thanked me for it.** That fine chick is the biggest problem in my life right now. **No you are the problem let her go. I hope you didn't think about marrying her.** What was I supposed to think? **You were supposed to be a player suck the honey and let her go.** Do you realize I have just lost seven thousand dollars you moron? **The way you are going you are bound to lose more money. My name is Charles Chiyangwa I am trying to make you a player.** No I am the real Charles Chiyangwa and I do not want to be a player. Look I am going in there and she will get rid of you. When she does her job you will be gone forever never to return. **Okay I am leaving just**

for now. I will sneak in and make decisions for you when you least expect it. Okay go ahead and live your boring life. You know I am thinking about things most men want to say to their women, but they never have the balls to say. Like I wish my hooker can train my wife how to have sex. God she knows a lot more about what to do than her lazy ass. She just lays there and let me do all the work. If it was not for the kids I would divorce her lazy ass now. Thank god for mistresses. I could have died of sexual boredom a long time ago. Look I am tired of you thinking like that. I am going to walk in there and you will be history. I want to live a normal life without saying all those things you put in my head. **I never put anything in your head fool. You were already crazy before I got here. Somehow now I have to help you get your money back.** No stay out of this I will fix it myself. **I want my boobs back. I will get them back one way or the other. I want my boobs back. I do not care about what you say I will get them back one way or the other.** Look they are not my boobs. I paid for them and

I am entitled to hold them by the contract. **I hate to break it to you. She was white trash before you paid for those boobs. She fucked every drug dealer out there for free. I meant it as a one night stand. You were supposed to spent fifty bucks not seven thousand fool.** She is not white trash. You think a millionaire can fall for white trash. White people know each other. **Obviously they do not know each other well. I can collect a thousand signatures of people she slept with easily.** Fuck you mother-fucker I am not going to sit here and listen to your bullshit! I then realize I have been talking to myself. That is scary. In the end I do not go in to get the help I need.

CHAPTER FIVE

Fake abs or fake boobs who cares?

Obviously I have had a lot on my mind lately. It's summer time so it makes sense to go to the beach and blow off some steam. The only problem is that my body has two pack abs and cannot gunner any attention from the ladies. Last time I went to the beach I got some attention from women. They were all asking me about the kind of diet I was on. I wasn't on any diet then and now. I am just skinny. Most women looked at me and told me they wish they had my body. That is not good for a guy. I am supposed to be the protector. How can I be the protector when most girls can pick me up like a feather? I remember one time a girl picked me up and kissed me while my feet were dangling in her arms. I do not care what people say it felt good. It is an experience most guys will never have.

My mind starts racing to find a way to make my beach experience worthwhile. A bunch of crazy ideas come up. The most practical is to visit my friend Steve. He is a special effects expert that I met at a party in the Hollywood hills. Steve is a typical nerd. He walks talks and dresses like a nerd. When Steve started talking about his line of work we immediately struck a friendship. I later visited his shop where they make prosthetic masks for the movies. It is a special effects company like no other. The day I got to visit him at his shop he had told me he was alone. He started showing me around the shop and suddenly a monster burst out from the corner. I jumped and held on to Steve for safety. I was so scared I was ready to get out of there. It turns out Steve was at work with his hot girlfriend who seemed amused at my reaction. Why do people have so much fun in pranking me? It seems like I have a sign on my forehead that says PRANK ME. It was quite an experience hanging out with Steve at his shop. I cannot get much work done with such a hot girl around. I asked Steve about it. His answer was that it gets his juices flowing. A girl that hot gets my juices flowing too.

I sent Steve a text to see if he can give me a prosthetic six pack, and a nice chest to shine at the beach. He laughs at first then he tells me he can do it. We set it up the next day for three hours in the morning. At six in the morning I am at Steve's shop ready for my instant makeover. I have to strip to my underwear to the amusement of Steve's girlfriend, who is constantly giggling while looking at me. I like to believe the African package is very different from an American one. I cannot tell whether she is laughing at me or just excited to see a half-naked guy. She may have been laughing at me because it is a crazy idea. After three hours of work I look in the mirror and I have a six pack. I have a well-built body sizzling with sex appeal for the ladies. Steve's girlfriend complements my appearance and that makes me smile. She pokes my abs and giggles again. Steve assures me that I can get into the water and do anything I wanted to do. This is the best shape of my life. I am ready to go meet some ladies at the beach. Steve's girlfriend spanks my ass as a sendoff. I stand there for a second hoping she hits my ass again. A good start to the day. I look in the mirror and I am the sexiest man alive.

I hit the beach and the results are instant. For the first time in my life I see girls looking at me like a piece of meat. They are offering me all kinds of stupid stuff so I can stop and talk to them. It feels like a dream. This to me is heaven on earth. As my instant celebrity on the beach grows it also attracts haters. A six foot giant weight lifting enthusiast walks towards me with a smile. He is impressed with my abs. He keeps looking at his own abs and then looking at mine. "I have been trying to get this kind of a six pack for years, he said. "You inspire me my man", he continues to shower me with praises. At this point I am getting uncomfortable. He asks me where I go to the gym. I tell him 24 hour fitness and he looks really surprised. He then asks me who my trainer is. I hesitate for a few seconds. I did not expect anyone to ask me that question. I told him Bob Johnson. That is the name that came to my head. He immediately starts checking the name on his iPhone with immense interest. He shakes his head with a little smile full of disappointment. He knows they are not real right away. He moves the hand of the girl holding me from behind and pokes my abs. He becomes really angry and pulls out a small piece of my abs. "Cheater I can crash you right now", he raises his voice getting ready to fight me. About six girls start pleading with him to let me go. He takes out a blow torch from his bag and lights it up. All I can hear is girls screaming very loud. He moves the blow torch towards me threatening to melt my abs away. He orders me to leave the beach immediately. Apparently he is mad that I have fake abs and he endures grueling workouts all the time. To him I am a cheater who deserves to melt. He calls me a lazy ass. The girls start laughing at me. That's why it is always important to leave while you are on top. Nobody leaves bikini clad girls playing alone on the beach. It never gets old. You might think I have seen it all but you still want to see some more.

Steve is not available to remove the prosthetics so I have to get help from his girlfriend. Under normal circumstances this is a piece of cake for me. A hot girl touching my body and pulling fake abs off my stomach is a good deal. I had to put additional stuff in certain areas, just to make me feel better about myself. I now have to explain to Steve's girlfriend why I need time for myself. Hopefully she will understand. I tickle very easy and giggle when certain parts of my body are touched by a girl. Things you do not want people to know.

CHAPTER SIX

Sling shot justice at The Grove.

Before we left Hooters I instructed Mike to go back in and lie to Taylor's sister Lauren. Mike told her she is next up for a contract. He told her we will come back to her with details. That turned out to be a very smart move. Whenever I needed details about Taylor her sister provided them. She provided me with information about her new boyfriend Trevor. Trevor is a young executive who works for an international corporation. He is a celebrity wannabe and a male socialite. Trevor drives around in a yellow Ferrari convertible. Lauren also told me about their next date at the Grove. The Grove is a 575,000 square foot retail and entertainment complex in the Fairfax district in Los Angeles. The complex has a shot tram ride that carries tourists from the farmer's market section through the shopping and dining areas. She told me all the details including the time of their arrival and reservations for lunch. I told my boy Mike and we got there three hours before they arrived. We set the place up to shut the date down. Mike brought his friend a bouncer at a local night club. I paid him one hundred bucks and told him what to do.

I can see the couple moving from the parking structure, into the main walkway leading to the shopping complex. The mood is romantic as they walk on a path to their reserved restaurant. The bouncer moves into action in this busy area full of people. Making it look like an accident he uses his shoulder to knock Trevor down. During the commotion he pulls out a spray bottle, and sprays Trevor as if to help him with the summer heat. It happens so quick by the time he says no to the spray he has already been sprayed. I bought the spray bottle in Hollywood and filled it with water and ice. I also added a stink and itchy solution bought on the internet. The special solution will make his skin itchy in five minutes or less. When he starts scratching it will stink badly. People have to be at least twenty feet away not to smell him. The bouncer sprays him good while he is down on the ground. He helps Trevor up and apologizes for the accident. The couple continues to walk towards the pond and make a left crossing the tram tracks. They stop at a concession stand selling sunglasses. The two lovebirds go into Victoria's secret to collect some shopping done over the phone. This is a nerve wrecking moment because I thought Victoria Secret would be the last place they visit. I have to make some minor adjustments to the plan over the phone with Mike and the bouncer. They finally settle at the outside patio of the restaurant to eat. His white shirt is a little wet but otherwise okay. Trevor starts scratching and soon after the stench begins to spread. An old couple close to them moves to another table in an effort to escape the smell. I leave for the parking lot where I flatten two of the front tires of his Ferrari. By the time I come back he has gotten rid of the sprayed shirt and put on a see through female top. The top is part of the order they collected earlier from the Victoria's Secret Store. Trevor is obviously secure with his manhood. He is determined to go through with the date. The itching does not stop. The stench is getting better but he keeps scratching like a drug addict. He finally had enough and makes a quick dash to his Ferrari for a plan B I guess. Little did he know that his ability to use money and seek help nearby has been thwarted? I know at some point he has to come back to Taylor with plan B.

I move in on Taylor making it look like a chance meeting. She is surprised to see me. She immediately starts talking about her new boyfriend. Like millions of dumped people around the world, I am happy to see my ex-girlfriend dating again. I convince her to see a new small blue shark they have in the pond. She refuses at first but I insist telling her it is the Grove's biggest attraction to date. She finally agrees and we walk to the edge of the pond, the side directly opposite the movie theatres.

When we get there I know exactly where she is going to end up according to the plan. I do not care how Mike does it. I just want him to get her in the water or at least wet. We move closer and closer to the edge of the pond, as I point to where the shark is deep in the water. She takes off her shoes and sits on the marble ridge surrounding the pond. The reason for her taking off her shoes baffles me. It certainly is a good move way better for my plans. I think Taylor feels sorry for me so she wants to make me feel better. I feel great knowing that she's is about to take a dip. Suddenly I hear the splash and when I wipe my eyes Taylor is in the water. Mike did such a good job I almost did not see him. Apparently Mike used a walking stick to push her over. She stands up in the water furious and confused. To me it looks like a bad wet t-shirt contestant. I try to help her out of the water but she is visibly mad. She walks out by herself. As I walk her back to the patio of the restaurant Trevor shows up. He wants to know what is happening. In my mind I am like do not mess with me rich boy. He looks at me like he is about to attack me. Taylor tells him that she slipped at the edge of the pond, and that I have nothing to do with it. Yeah I have absolutely nothing to do with it. I can't be held responsible for girls showing off their breasts wet t-shirt contest style. Taylor is dripping wet and Trevor is still scratching like a rural meth addict. This is top of the line fun. It is clear they need new clothes so they slowly walk into the closest clothing store. There goes the rich boy peeing on the poor guy. It really makes me angry. I get hold of myself and plot the next move.

I run to the parking lot and take the escalators to the third floor of the parking structure. I place myself in a position right in front of the store with a clear shot. I take out my sling shot. It looks just like the one used in angry birds my favorite video game. My sling shot is a very portable one that I can easily hide in my pocket. It is a deadly weapon when I want it be. Whenever I use it at unsuspecting enemies they always look around, and go to the nearest building threatening to sue them.

They usually have no idea what hit them. I am literally going to bring a multi-millionaire to his knees. None of my friends in America know that in Africa I was a sling shot sharp shooter. One stone for one bird was my motto. My record is one thousand stones for one thousand birds. I never missed with a sling shot. I am not going to miss a guy abusing my boobs. I have two pebbles in hand and I load one on the sling.

The couple walks out of the store wearing brand new clothes. The two love birds stroll towards the water fountain, and turn towards me walking slowly to the entrance of the restaurant. She is walking slightly ahead of him wearing new clothes. I have a few seconds to execute, and it is a piece of cake for a sling shot veteran like me. I quickly pull and release the pebble landing on Trevor's knee as they walk to the restaurant. That pebble stops him from moving that leg. Quickly I let loose another beautiful beach pebble and it lands on the other knee. In five seconds he cannot move his legs. Before Taylor turns back I hit his stomach area with a bigger pebble. Taylor looks back and appears upset she urges him to walk faster. Trevor drops to his knees with a straight face. Taylor becomes excited about a pending proposal. She has her hands together, behaving like a girl waiting for a proposal in the middle of a shopping mall. Trevor tries to put on a brave face and smiles a little. That makes Taylor bubble with excitement waiting for those magic words. The magic words never come out of his mouth. Instead Trevor indicates he needs some help to get up. Taylor goes from excitement to disappointment in a split second. I can see Trevor trying to explain that he has been hit by something. It looks like she cannot believe him. Who can believe a guy saying he just got hit by stones falling from the sky. She probably thinks he just changed his mind on the proposal. They walk with Trevor's arm leaning on her shoulder. This date has to end and I want it to end right away. I run down to street level and hide in front of them. I mount the smallest pebble and hit him on the forehead. This time Trevor cries out. "What is wrong with you", exclaimed Taylor getting really impatient with her man. About a minute later a protruding bulge starts forming on his forehead. That definitely sent them home. My guy on the ground Mike is keeping me informed of all their actions as he is closer to them. After looking at his forehead Mike cannot hold it together. Trevor calls a limousine and they make their way out of the Grove. The date is over just like that. The Bouncer, Mike and me sit at the Grove and have lunch and drinks to celebrate. It is bitter sweet because at the end of the day I lost my money and she still has the boobs. Well if Trevor tries to kiss her the swelling on his forehead makes first contact.

CHAPTER SEVEN

These dead people are scandalous!

It is an ordinary Los Angeles day and I feel good for ruining Taylor's date. I have been yelled at for not driving one second after the traffic light turned green. I yelled back just keeping it a little under road rage volume. Then as young people like me often do, I walk into a bar. This is just to have a drink or two to collect my thoughts. I settle on the corner sofa overlooking the main bar entrance and order my first beer. Then suddenly a silhouette of a Hispanic girl with the most beautiful figure appears at the entrance. She sizzles with sex appeal just what I need while having my beer. She looks dark and dangerous yet very sexy. The first thing that comes to my mind when I see a girl like this is sex. As she walks into the light I realize she is gothic. I am mentioning it like it matters. It is like okay if she is gothic I am gothic too. Let's walk into the dark side of this bar. It did not stop me from wondering how she became gothic. How can a Latino girl sizzling with sex appeal have time to think about the dark side? I get the every girl has a black dress thing. Everybody looks good in black. Going all the way gothic is a little much. She stands there near the entrance as if looking for someone. She is wearing a way above the knee flare mini skirt, with studded boots up to just below the knee. She also wore the most revealing tank top God ever made.

She walks right up to me and explodes. "What are you doing here? What made you choose this day and this particular time to come and have a drink here? Tell me why?" she asks me coming close to my face. Talk about confused emotions. I do not know whether to be afraid or to challenge back. One thing for sure is that at this point I am sweating. My erect penis in one second shrunk back to its original size. I look confused and I am asking myself an obvious question. What have I got myself into this time? The confusion on my face says it all. Then she smiles and slowly starts laughing at me for getting scared. She gives me the look and tells me her name is Maria Lopez. My excuse for getting scared is that I heard about gothic chicks killing people in Los Angeles bars. Where does that excuse come from? Your guess is as good as mine. It feels real and I say it with confidence. Then I remembered seeing it in a movie. Before long I am buying beer and having a good time. It is fun listening to stories from her perspective. After a few beers I can sense something happening. Maria slowly stands up looking right straight into my eyes biting her lips. To tell the truth I do not know how to respond. The longer she plays with her lips the more I know what is expected of me. I slowly stand up looking right straight into her eyes. Maria Lopez slaps me hard and grabs my collar with both hands. She gives me the deepest and most passionate French kiss. She pulls back looking directly into my eyes. I can see the bartender shaking his head. At this point my cheek is burning from being slapped. I feel the urge to rub it or something. I can hear the voice in my head saying I am not a punk. I am hardcore. Bring it on babe! I certainly do not want to look like a wimp. I try to look tough like a gangster. I have a big question for her. Why did you slap me bitch? That did not come out of my mouth. I imagine myself asking a thousand times but in the end I do not ask. Now I remember three guys walked out of the bar when she appeared at the entrance. Maybe they are regulars who know things I do not know.

Before you know it Maria and I end up at my apartment. I put on some slow music, and switch on the red light I have not used in a longtime. I sit on the bed looking at her across my bedroom. Maria is looking at herself in the mirror. If I looked this good I would spend time looking at myself in the mirror too. She starts walking like she is on the runway letting me see a little of her ass on the swing. She finally stands in front of me giving me that sultry look. She makes her way to the home theatre system and plugs in her iPod. Industrial Goth type music starts playing, and she stands there kind of trying to collect herself. Maria suddenly looks menacing like I have done something wrong. She holds me up by the collar with one hand, like she is about to beat the shit out of me. At this point I make up my mind not to do anything. I am not going to resist this goddess. I am just going to let her bit me up and have sex. I will definitely call the cops later. As I am thinking about that she gives me a kiss and slaps me again. Maria pushes me on the bed while taking her top off leaving her bra on. She works her magic like a pro.

Afterwards I am relaxing on the bed wondering whether to ask about the slapping. My decision this time is easy because I am convinced I have met the goddess of sex. If the goddess of sex has to slap me so she can work her magic so be it. It does not kill does it? Then she starts telling me that for some reason she is always mad at something. She does not know why. So she takes all the anger and madness into sex. I am thinking that is a good way to take care of anger management issues. This is something the people can use to make this world a better place. I have no problem with that. I believe her. I have never been fucked while my cheeks are burning before. I guess there is a first time for everything.

We joke around and I call her mad Latina, the nickname sticks in my head. From now on she is mad Latina to me and she does not mind the nickname at all. She prefers to be called Bad Latina though. Maria starts frequently shouting "I am a Bad Latina with a capital B". She tells me about her belief in numerology as a religion. I do not ask any further questions because it just sounds complicated to me. Bad Latina hates the number two. She also believes in the paranormal, and found it relaxing to make routine walks through the local cemetery. I did not like it at first until I had sex on top of some girl's gravestone. It is a threesome I will never forget. That is the first time I ever had a threesome with a girl dead or alive. Apparently the dead like it because it is very boring being dead. They can use a little bit of action once in a while.

To say I am having sex with her is a lie. She is having sex with me. I can only do things I am told to do. She is completely in control of everything from start to finish. As all the emotions begin to settle, I notice that she has small breasts. They are like a size A or something. I now understand why she is always mad. I would be mad too. It's like having a one inch penis. That makes a guy mad no doubt about that. For Bad Latina the goddess of sex the size of her boobs is not an issue. She is the only one exempt from that requirement. She is always dressed provocatively. God must have known I love eye candy. I have more erections in this relationship than I have had in my whole life. The bad thing is not all erections lead to sex. A bunch of them end up as very painful blue balls. Those make you appreciate walking freely.

Taylor robbed me of my savings in broad daylight. It is clear that I did not know enough about her at all. So I took it upon myself to do some digging around. I visited some of her friends and family. She had mentioned some of them in our brief relationship if you can call it that. I found out that she is an out of work stunt woman. She was fired from a stunt team on a TV show for doing drugs on set. The day she got fired the actress she was supposed to do stunts for did a better job herself. She was high as a kite on the day of her firing. She did not even know that she had been fired because she went to work the next day. Security barred her from entering the studio lot. Basically she is a crack head or lack of a better word white trash. She surely is a master at covering it up. Who in their right mind gives up such a top job for crack? I cannot believe I gave boobs to a crack head. She looked like a princess. Maybe I do not know what a princess looks like in real life. Well she felt good when I touched her. What was I thinking or did I think at all? Here is what I think happened. I looked at her and had that first intense erection, and then everything went haywire. Now I want my boobs back. I want them back. Bad Latina deserves them. She is not a crack head. Bad Latina does not need any drugs at all. She is naturally high I think. She likes dead people and the dark side whatever she calls it. I do not judge.

Never in a million years did I think I would be watching an old movie in a cemetery partying. Well she took me to this event at the Hollywood Forever Cemetery. It feels like you are watching a movie with famous dead people. You're sitting there alive and they are laying there deceased. I felt a hand in my pants. I am thinking these dead people are scandalous. I am with my girlfriend hallo! It's kind of weird if you think about it. I never thought I would get excited about the day of the dead? Well it happens when you fall in love.

There is no doubt in my mind that I am in love with Bad Latina. This is supposed to be the happiest time of my life. Well Bad Latina gives me a different kind of love. The kind of love I never experienced before. There is something new every day. One day both my hands and feet are tied to the bed as she works her magic. Other days she uses a whip all in the name of sexual magic. She opened me up to a whole new world of sexual pleasure. Sometimes she plays Goth music which I never appreciated before she played it under the right circumstances.

The events a few weeks earlier keep coming back into my head. It bothers me that money I worked so hard for got lost in that way. You cannot even tell your best friend about it. How do you even start? I paid for a boob job and the chick dumped me a few days later. That makes me the laughing stock of the whole crew. The result is I am occasionally sad. Bad Latina asks me about it and every time I lie to her. I am tired of the lies and I am going to tell her the truth now.

I let her know my plan is to find a way to enforce the contract. I suggested the idea of starting a business, and employing Taylor as a secretary. That is so I can have access to enforce the contract. Bad Latina nods her head in agreement. That never happened before. I have finally got Bad Latina to stop talking and listen to me. Then things suddenly change. She puts on a face that usually let me know I am in big trouble. She accused me of being an African trying to have two wives. She also accused me of trying to cheat making her number two. Bad Latina let me know my plan is not going to happen because it involves the number two. Her plan is the one going ahead. All I have to do is listen to her and follow instructions. I have no choice in the matter.

Sure enough by the end of the day she comes up with the most ridiculous plan I ever heard. She reads through the contract, and quickly concludes it is null and void. Then she tells me the last clause: removal by force or coercion can be enforced outside the court system in the underground. She knows people who can help us out. She tells me about this one doctor who owes her a big favor, after she saved his ass from going to prison. Doctor Graham is his name. Bad Latina let me know about the doctor's history right away. Doctor Graham as a young man was a television news anchor at one of the top television stations. He was fired for routinely reading his own news during critical coverage at the network. With no job and fascinated by beauty he went back to college to be a plastic surgeon. He graduated and went into private practice. For the first few years he was the most successful plastic surgeon in Beverly Hills. Then the dark forces returned when his marriage ran into troubles. His wife divorced him. He tricked her into surgery where he removed her breast implants, and replaced them with ones made of water packets. Her breasts make a sound every time she tries to run or walk fast. That's how he lost his practicing license and became a huge hit on the internet underground. He still does surgery for cheap in the underground. He makes as much money as he used to make. The fact that he used to operate on famous people works in his favor. Ordinary people flock to him to get plastic surgery for cheap. There was a period where he had some substance abuse issues. He has been clean for a few years now she explains. He volunteers for the Beverly Hills Fire Department. He has access to all their facilities.

Bad Latina is going to arrange a meeting with this doctor. The plan goes into effect shortly after that meeting. The thing is I do not know if I said yes to the plan. The plan seems to be going ahead. There is unusual enthusiasm from Bad Latina and I cannot figure it out. She explains it to me this way. "We will get this bitch and the doctor will remove the implants you paid for. Then you can give them to someone you like", she said. I figured it out right away. Bad Latina wants those boobs given to her. I realized my life will never be the same again until we get it done.

She set up a meeting with Dr. Graham at a strip club in the San Fernando Valley. "Why are we meeting him at a strip club?" I ask her. Bad Latina explains to me that he is now working underground. The strip club is where he gets most of his clients. She drives me to the club in the valley. We arrive and park outside the club. It is a normal Strip Club. We go inside and the doctor has his own special VIP area with body guards. We are searched for weapons, and I finally sit across the guy

I have to get to know real fast. The doctor and I shake hands and begin the talks. The first thing that comes to my mind is he looks trustworthy. This is someone you want to read the news to you every night. It does not take long into the conversation before I realize there has to be more to this man. The way he relates to the strippers is remarkable. Doctor Graham is a Caucasian man in his late forties early fifties. He still looks good for his age. Bad Latina leads the discussions. The doctor takes over on providing resources at his disposal to help make the plan a success. It is a straight forward case and the doctor says it shouldn't be a problem. He brags about being an expert in this sort of thing.

After the meeting with Dr Graham the ball is in our court. We have to locate Taylor and then contact the doctor. He gave us the most ideal places to make things easy. That helps a lot because we know places that can pose a danger to the plan. The doctor adds that he is doing all this for free. It is a way of saying thank you to Bad Latina for her help. The case could have sent him to prison for years. Bad Latina and the doctor have refused to talk about the details of that situation. She just says to me some things are better left unsaid. I have learnt not to push things with Bad Latina. They might end up in places you would rather not go. I zip my mouth and walk to the door while feasting on eye candy. I cannot stare at the girls although I want to. I have to be careful.

CHAPTER EIGHT

The end of the road for Taylor's big boobs?

We locate Taylor through her sister Lauren. I make a call to Doctor Graham and the plan gets active right away. The doctor gets a real ambulance from the Beverly Hills Fire Department. A fake ambulance mission and it does not look fishy at all. A real ambulance just up to no good you can say. It is up to my good. For the first time Beverly Hills is doing something for me. The ambulance is keeping a distance behind Taylor, after we found her car on Santa Monica Boulevard. Bad Latina and I are driving her Honda Civic behind the ambulance. At some point it crosses my mind we could have stayed home, and waited for the call for surgery. The adrenalin is too much; I cannot miss this for anything in the world. The only time you see this type of scenario is in a movie. The other time is when a third striker is being chased down by the police. They try to get away unsuccessfully before they are locked up for life. We are chasing a white Ford Taurus on Santa Monica Boulevard driving into West Hollywood. We pass West Hollywood into Beverly Hills. She is now aware someone is following her. On Camden drive she turns left all the way to Wilshire Boulevard. She makes a right on Wilshire then stops the car after half a block. Taylor runs into a nearby building.

The ambulance parks behind her car and we all file into the building. She does not wait for the elevator. She takes the stairs. The doctor and Bad Latina are ahead of me. The doctor urges me to speed up. Bad Latina remains silent she just looks at me with disdain. I know I have to step it up or my life is going to get interesting in the bedroom. The doctor says it is a good idea to visit the gym sometimes. Seriously I feel like a girl, well a girl is ahead of me. I feel like an older man, well an older man is running the stairs in front of me. The conclusion is that I feel like a useless piece of shit. An older man urging me to run the stairs does not look good in front of my girlfriend. One particularly embarrassing moment comes when the doctor asks, "Who is the man in the house?" That is a low blow for real. I try to tell him he has gone too far but I am out of breath. He thinks I said we have gone far enough. He points up the building to where she is. We get to the last floor where Taylor patiently waits for us to arrive. We find out pretty quickly that she has set up traps for us. Most of the offices on the top floors of this building are closed for renovations. Only a few offices are open on each floor. As we get to the hallway the doctor slips and goes down rolling over like a log. He cannot hold on to anything. Whatever he touches he ends up on the floor. He stepped on some kind of slippery substance. We have to figure out something quick or otherwise we are down one man.

A smartly dressed male clerk comes out to help him. We see them go into an office.

After a few minutes only the doctor emerges from the office. He is smartly dressed as the clerk that went in with him. He is ready to read you the news! We have no time to ask him what he has done. We have to move on. This is a huge building. I am now leading the pack as we walk around the hallways looking for Taylor. In a way I am trying to make up for my sloppy stairs debacle. All of a sudden all I remember is my head hitting the floor. Two people are turning me over and I am hearing "are you alright" over and over again. As I lift my head I can see that I tripped on a wire that runs across the hallway. They get me up and my genes are filled with fury to say the least.

My advice to Doctor Graham is to do a bad boob job on her so she looks like a freak. I want men to scream in shock when she opens them up. She is a good candidate for water packets in her boobs. We continue the search for Taylor in this maze of a floor. To keep us safe from traps, I found myself pushing a broom on the floor to catch anything suspicious. We appear to be going nowhere so we stop to strategize.

Bad Latina who is wearing black leggings and a black tank top bend over slowly to massage her feet. She rests her ass on the wall. While this is going on I try talking to the doctor, who is constantly looking at my girlfriend's ass. When the doctor blatantly stares at my girlfriend's ass it makes me wonder if I can trust him. I look over to Bad Latina wiggling her ass and making unbelievable movements. It does not take long for us to realize her ass is stuck to the wall. She is stuck on some type of glue. I try to pull her off the wall. The choices are either we cut part of the wall and duct tape it to her ass, or I cut part of her leggings off leaving her ass exposed. She is wearing one of those string thongs that do not cover much. This is one time I wish she is wearing granny panties. She opens her bag and pulls out a knife. She gives it to me to cut her leggings off the wall. My eyes almost pop out. This is not because of her amazing ass but the fact that she has a knife. I cut her leggings off the wall. She quickly pulls out some spandex booty shorts she works out in from her bag. I kind of instruct the doctor to look away but he does half way. She takes off the torn leggings and put on booty shorts. This is amazing stuff! I used to pay to see this sought of thing. I cannot help but laugh at my girl but she is visibly mad.

As we turn the corner in the hallway I cannot believe my eyes. Suddenly I can see Taylor walking right in front of us. We all tip toe towards her and I signal the doctor to grab her from behind. We get close and the doctor goes for it in cop like fashion. They both go down only to realize we got the wrong girl. I have never seen a girl that mad. It looks like one of us is getting killed or going to jail after this is all over. The doctor talks her out of calling the cops by offering Laker tickets.

We finally catch up with Taylor. This time we are sure because she turns around and we all clearly see her face. We all run after her and I get my cigar out ready to blow the poison dart. We get close enough and I have a clear shot. I blow the dart and hit her at the back of her neck. However she does not stop.

She continues running then opens the maintenance door and locks us out. We have to figure out a way to open the door. I have her incapacitated by the dart already. Opening the door proves harder that we all anticipated. As the minutes tick away we all know at some point the poison on the dart fades. Time is not on our side. We try all kinds of tricks and the door does not open. Bad Latina goes away for a couple of minutes and returns with a door buster. The one cops use to break down doors in raids. Apparently they have one here for small precision demolitions. She orders us out of the way as she hits the door a couple of times and it opens. We hesitantly move inside a room full of tools. As we all get to the window I cannot believe my eyes. There is a rope tied to the window. She waited for us to emerge. As soon as she sees us she gives us the middle finger disappearing into the afternoon crowd. Silence dominates our frustrated faces as anger sets in. The breeze did manage to cool us down from the running. Bad Latina stands near the window shouting some expletives at

Taylor who has already left. She challenges her to a fist fight next time they meet. Wherever the meeting happens I need to be there. Just to avoid a dead body.

The reason why the dart did not work is because it took long to open the maintenance door. She was down in the room and did something crazy. She got up and made her escape. When she sees me again she will know what the dart is all about. That worries me a lot. It is always better with unassuming prey. Obviously she will think it will make her do the same thing. That is where the surprise element of the dart will kick in. If ever I get close to her with Bad Latina, I risk seeing her being strangled in front of me. It might be necessary to dart Bad Latina under special circumstances to keep things under control. Just the thought of that happening scares me. She can make me suffer in the bedroom? You do not want to mess with bedroom action.

My phone rings and I immediately realize Taylor is calling me. She now wants to give me my money back. Allegedly her rich boyfriend Trevor is supposed to pay me. She uses the word cute describing Trevor. Okay we will see how cute he is after I am done with him. Taylor is going to give me my money back and keep the boobs for him. I am probably going to take the money and let it go. The idea that some rich guy is going to be the king maker infuriates me. This is not about money. I am not a whore. This is about principles. My girlfriend wants the boobs. I feel the urge to get even with this guy that messed up my life with Taylor. This is a perfect storm of events and emotions. I am going ahead with the original plan.

She tells me to meet her in Beverly Hills. Her boyfriend is holding an event to benefit homeless teenagers at the Beverly Hilton Hotel. According to her the Beverly Hilton Hotel is the best place to do the transaction. According to me it is a perfect place to maximize embarrassment for Trevor. For Bad Latina it is like let's go in and get the bitch under the knife. We decided it is a good idea to launch an ambush. We will move in during the event as opposed to after the event in their private hotel room.

We contact the doctor again so he can have everything set for the showdown. It is a piece of cake for him, he is known at the hotel because of the many high profile clients he used to have. The plan is in full swing. Our ambulance parks a block away waiting for the signal to pick up the patient for surgery. The three of us all go into the hotel to execute the plan. It is going to be a summer surprise. All systems go at 7pm.

I am dressed in a grey suit with an off white shirt and grey shoes. Bad Latina refused to change course and is wearing an all-black outfit. Bad Latina has heavy makeup on but with less piercings on her face. The signature red lipstick stands out. She has shiny metal studs all through her outfit. Doctor Graham is wearing a navy blue suit. The doctor looks comfortable because this is his neighborhood. He grew up in Beverly Hills. He remembers well when he attended Beverly Hills High School.

That's pretty much as Beverly Hills as you can get to me. That gives me a lot of confidence in the mission. I know we are in safe hands.

We arrive at the hotel and immediately hit the green room where everybody is having drinks. But before we get through to the green room, we have to pass through the reception area, manned by a flamboyant man who has a certain way of talking. When he looks at me it feels like he is judging my clothes. He is very nice he let us in. He does not seem to approve of Bad Latina's outfit though. The love birds where not difficult to spot. Trevor is dressed and looks like Brad Pitt. I cannot help but think she is getting laid by a Brad Pitt lookalike and she has fake boobs. Some of these lookalikes are just as good as the real thing you know. It reminds me of the Halle Berry lookalike I slept with. It felt like I had sex with the real deal.

It is time to break up the party. As they separate to attend to different groups of people, I move into position so I can get a clean shot. I get my darts out with a cigar in my mouth ready to blow. Before you know it I have a clean shot of pretty boy from behind. He will never know what hit him. I blow my cigar and hit him right at the back of the neck. He holds his neck in slight discomfort. Taylor is on the other end busy chatting and laughing her way in high society. She does not have a clue of our presence yet. I know as soon as she becomes aware of what has happened to her boyfriend, she will be aware of our presence. She is expecting us to wait for them in their hotel room. I know she will quickly make her way to the door. At the door is where I am waiting for her, with a cigar in my mouth ready to blow. The three of us position ourselves at or near the door. We are waiting for the mayhem to begin.

I have the cigar in my mouth ready to blow on a clear shot. We are hoping to pull this off preferably unnoticed. I am standing at the door. Doctor Graham and Bad Latina are on either end of the door. We are just waiting patiently. It seems like the longest fifteen minutes of my life. I know I have hit Trevor for sure. Something has to happen unless the dart is making him do something quiet. That is a possibility. In that case this whole mission will fail. The look on Bad Latina's face says it all. She's got what the hell is going on face? That is the last thing you need from her in this type of situation. When that face shows up in our relationship things do not turn out well for me. At least she gave me a chance after all. She is my girl and all this is for her.

The doctor has given up because he gets a drink from the waiter. As soon as he holds the glass of wine the noise starts from the back of the room. That is the position I last saw Trevor. Doctor Graham quickly puts back the glass of wine on the waiter's tray. I know we are now in business. He gives me his trademark look. That makes me slightly smile because I know what is about to happen. I can hear a loud voice singing or performing karaoke. I look over and for sure I see Trevor singing looking like he is very drunk. I can see Trevor hugging and kissing other people's wives. He even kisses a man on the cheek. One of the executives look confused. "What just happened?" I hear him ask a friend next to him. The friend reluctantly says, "I think he planted one on you". The top executive did not seem to mind the kiss. The executive that had his wife French kissed sprang into action. He positions himself in front of the singing seemingly intoxicated Trevor. He appears to move to his singing raising his hands as if encouraging him. Then suddenly he violently puts his glass shoe into Trevor's groin. That stops the music. Pretty boy music goes silent.

The party DJ continues to play music. At this point Taylor realizes that something is wrong. She starts to make her way to Trevor while scanning the room for the usual suspects. That is when she locks eyes with Bad Latina. Bad Latina whistles to let me know the game is on. As she makes her way to the door, I keep hiding behind people so she cannot see me. I land right behind her as she walks straight to the door. With my clear shot position achieved I blow one right away. I see her hold her neck and wipe a minute spec of blood. As soon as she holds the door she collapses. Bad Latina smiles at this welcome development. I loudly ask everyone if there is a doctor in the house. Doctor Graham steps in and Bad Latina also jumps in saying she is a nurse. I pretend to call 911 and told everybody the ambulance is on its way. The 911 call I place is to our guys with the ambulance one block away. The doctor pretends to attend to her a couple of doors down from the green room. The ambulance sirens starts going. At this point we carry her to the elevator down to the ground floor. At the reception the flamboyant man comes running and asks the doctor what happened. The doctor tells him she drank too much. "It happens a lot around here", says the man with a smirk on his face. We manage to put Taylor into the ambulance without incidence.

Doctor Graham and I ride in the back of the ambulance with Taylor driving to his office aka the hospital. Bad Latina is driving behind us by herself. We do not want her in the ambulance, because that can cause a calm situation to be very unpredictable. As planned we arrive at Doctor Graham's office without incident. Taylor woke up with Bad Latina at her bedside. Doctor Graham and I walk into the room and realize that she has been chained to the bed complete with leg irons. We just look at each other surprised by her extreme actions. I cannot believe it but I understand it. The doctor takes the leg irons away and tells us to wait two hours for surgery to begin. The wait was in part to allow the dart poison to subside or be neutralized. We get an armed security guard to secure her. Bad Latina has to get ready in the next room for a smooth transfer. As Taylor lay on the bed she appears to be sleeping peacefully. The security guard has the gun pointed at her when she makes a movement. I cannot help but think soon she will be a white girl with small boobs again. The world will be a better place.

The three of us leave the room to go eat together. We eat at a nearby restaurant to avoid wasting any more time. We all return to Doctor Graham's office to set everything up for the surgeries. I put Bad Latina at ease on a bed in a separate room. The doctor tells her she can take a nap while he operates on Taylor. The doctor's assistants for hire arrive on time to help out. They look like strippers in nurse uniforms to me. I cannot tell whether they are real or not.

The doctor opens the locked door to Taylor's room. The security guard lay naked on the bed with his hands tied behind his back. His mouth is sealed with duct tape and he is only able to make mow sounds. There are a couple of used condoms on the bed making it obvious what transpired in the room. Taylor is nowhere to be seen. I instruct the shocked doctor's assistants to wait for us in the reception area. We both look at each other with a sense of resignation. We decide not to untie the security guard, and try figure out how to tell Bad Latina. The doctor excused his assistants and he takes a nap in his comfortable office chair. I just lay down on the office sofa wondering why.

In my sleep begins a dream that feels vivid and real. I am in Paris France on Shanzelize Avenue doing some shopping. The African American girl with the voice of an angel appears to walk towards me. She looks more angelic in her beauty better than before. As my mind wonders how I can say hi given what happened in our previous meeting, I just smile. Suddenly there is noise and commotion. I see six little people wearing white rain coats running towards me. Another group of six little people with white raincoats comes from behind me. They all hold me down and turn me over to face the girl with the voice of an angel. She is smiling as she stands over me. I can see her panties as she slowly lowers herself to get good aim at my face. The little people start chanting in unison. Do it! Do it! Do it! Do it! I try to scream but nothing comes out. My mouth opens but no sound comes out. I try to make movements but my body does not move. Her crotch slowly moves closer to my face and I suddenly wake up. I am breathing hard and sweating at the same time. I wish this was a wet dream fucking the girl with the voice of an angel! I can see Doctor Graham is up. It is time to figure out what to do.

"What is taking so long?" a sleepy Bad Latina asks. We both look at each other with no idea how to respond.

www.ingramcontent.com/pod-product-compliance
Lightning Source LLC
LaVergne TN
LVHW091009080826
845145LV00003B/1197

* 9 7 8 0 9 8 4 8 8 3 3 0 1 *